TIS THE CONTENTS

DECEMBER 2024

CEO & Founder

Paulette Henson

Founder's Note

Dear Readers,

Celebrating the Essence of Black Womanhood: A Journey Through Words
In the vibrant tapestry of literature, Black women authors have woven threads of resilience, wisdom, and beauty, crafting narratives that illuminate the rich tapestry of their experiences. BWA Magazine proudly celebrates the profound impact of Black women authors, whose voices resonate across generations, continents, and cultures.

Empowering Narratives: Black women authors stand at the forefront of literary excellence, fearlessly exploring themes of identity, heritage, and empowerment. Their stories delve deep into the complexities of life, offering insights, inspiration, and hope to readers worldwide. From powerful memoirs to captivating fiction, each page of BWA Magazine is adorned with the brilliance of their storytelling.
Unveiling Untold Stories: Within the pages of BWA Magazine, hidden histories are unearthed, and silenced voices are amplified. Black women authors courageously confront societal injustices, challenge stereotypes, and reclaim their narratives with unwavering determination. Their words serve as beacons of truth, illuminating the path towards a more inclusive and equitable world.

A Platform for Expression: BWA Magazine provides a platform for Black women authors to share their stories, celebrate their achievements, and connect with a diverse audience of readers. Through thought-provoking interviews, insightful essays, and captivating book features, BWA Magazine honors the brilliance and resilience of Black women in literature.

Inspiring Future Generations: As torchbearers of literary excellence, Black women authors inspire future generations to dream, create, and thrive. Their words serve as catalysts for change, sparking conversations, and igniting movements for social justice and equality. BWA Magazine is dedicated to uplifting and empowering the voices of Black women authors, ensuring that their legacies endure for generations to come.

Join the Celebration: Embark on a literary journey like no other with BWA Magazine. Discover the diverse voices, powerful stories, and transformative wisdom of Black women authors who continue to shape the landscape of literature. With each issue, BWA Magazine celebrates the essence of Black womanhood and honors the enduring legacy of Black women in literature.

BLACK WOMEN AUTHORS
Supporting & Empowering Through Literature

Black women authors have long been at the forefront of literary excellence, using their powerful voices to inspire and empower readers worldwide. Through their captivating storytelling, they shed light on the diverse experiences and struggles faced by Black women, making their narratives not only relatable but also transformative. These authors fearlessly explore the intersections of race, gender, and identity, challenging societal norms and dismantling stereotypes. Their works serve as a source of inspiration, offering a mirror for readers to see themselves and their struggles reflected in the pages. From thought-provoking fiction to insightful memoirs and empowering self-help books. Black women authors leave an indelible mark on the literary landscape, instilling a sense of pride and self-acceptance in their readers. Their words are a rallying cry for change, empowering generations to come and reminding us all of the strength and resilience that lies within.

Propel Your Organization To Level Execllence

With over 23 years of experience in transforming lives, Dr. Kim is a passionate advocate for well-being and excellence. She specializes in guiding individuals, teams, and organizations to uncover their purpose, amplify unique skills, and enhance productivity. Partner with Dr. Kim to empower your organization to reach its peak performance and achieve remarkable success!

DOCTORKSD EVOLVED

Life Coach | Author | Keynote Speaker
Advanced Grief Recovery Specialist | Physician

Dr. Kimberly Smith-Dauterive, M.D.

Dr. Kim has over 23 years of experience motivating, nurturing, healing, and transforming lives as she strives to achieve her motto of "healing the mind, body and spirit." She guides individuals, group, and organizations in finding their purpose and amplifying their natural talents and skills to raise them to their highest potential.

Dr. Kim founded the DoctorKSD Evolved brand with a mission to empower individuals trapped by life's challenges. By providing essential tools, DoctorKSD Evolved helps individuals overcome past hurts, break free from negatively inherited mindsets, and move beyond antiquated traditions. For INDIVIDUALS, our goal is to assist you in reaching your full potential to achieve the exceptional life you deserve. For BUSINESSES, we focus on nurturing individuals who are poised to elevate your organization to new levels of excellence, ensuring your team is equipped to drive innovation and success.

LET'S WORK TOGETHER

Need a Life Coach, Team Building Coach, or Keynote Speaker? Contact us now at **info@doctorksd.com**. We can't wait to help propel you to your next level of excellence.

Live Life With Purpose On Purpose

"No one but God knew I needed this. During this time I was able to release the grief I held onto for over a year. Dr. Kim listened without judgment, but she also helped me to let go of that dark cloud that hindered me for so long. I am forever grateful I was able to let go of so much. I feel so much better!" ~ N.H

Your Life & Wellness Coach

Workshops | Conferences | Confidence Building | Virtual Events
Panel Discussions | College & High School Graduations | Support Groups

DOCTORKSD.COM

Follow @DoctorKSD_evolved

INFO@DOCTORKSD.COM

Tips on Marketing Your Book

Writing a book is a monumental achievement, but getting your masterpiece into the hands of readers can be an equally daunting task. Whether you're a self-published author or traditionally published, effective marketing is crucial to your book's success. Here are some practical tips to help you promote your book and reach your target audience.

Know Your Audience

Before you dive into marketing, it's essential to identify your target audience. Who are the readers most likely to enjoy your book? Consider age, gender, interests, and reading habits. Understanding your audience will enable you to tailor your marketing strategies effectively.

Create a Strong Author Brand

Your author brand is your identity in the literary world. It encompasses your writing style, your voice, and your values. Invest time in establishing a professional website and maintain consistent branding across all your social media platforms. Use your brand to connect with readers on a personal level, sharing insights into your writing process, inspirations, and more.

Organize Virtual Book Tours

With the rise of virtual events, book tours have become more accessible. Partner with bloggers, influencers, and bookstagrammers to host virtual events where you can discuss your book, answer questions, and engage with readers. Consider hosting giveaways or contests to create buzz and excitement around your release.

Host Events and Signings

If you're comfortable with public speaking, consider hosting book signings or readings at local bookstores, libraries, or community centers. These events can help you connect with readers directly and provide a platform for you to share your passion for your book.

Network with Other Authors

Building relationships with fellow authors can be incredibly beneficial. Collaborate on projects, cross-promote each other's works, or participate in joint events. A supportive writing community can significantly enhance your book's visibility and lead to new opportunities.

Happy Holidays!

MISS-ADVENTURES LOVE COACHING
EMPOWERING WOMEN ON ALL ASPECTS OF LOVE

Stephanie is a Certified Master Life Coach, the CEO of Miss-Adventures, LLC, three-time #1 Bestselling author, and #1 New Release. Stephanie's mission is empowering women on all aspects of love. She strongly believes in the power of prayer and affirmations to ignite and create the love, health, wealth, success, family, abundance, relationships, and prosperity we want in our lives. Stephanie is a podcaster, public speaker, published writer—over 250 articles between hubpages, Paired Life and Elephant Journal. She has also been a guest on multiple radio and podcast shows. Stephanie has been mentoring women for over 26-plus years and offers in-person and virtual sessions.

STEPHANIE BAILEY

BENEFITS OF SELF-LOVE:

- Personal Growth
- Using your voice—not being afraid to speak up.
- Confronting your fears.
- Empowering yourself through forgiveness—to release being a victim.
- And more…

"Stephanie is an exceptionally valuable expert on relationship advice. Over the years her wisdom and guidance have been at the core of my personal growth on my journey. xoxoxo Love you!"

— NANCY G., COLORADO

CONTACT:

323-332-9976
MISS-ADVENTURES.COM

MISS-ADVENTURES.COM

Happy
Holidays

FREE EVEN
UNSEEN TO
UNSTOPPABLE
ESSENTIAL STRATEGIES DESIGNED TO CREATE
REMARKABLE WOMEN WHO SHINE!
Launching January 7th, 2025
with Host
Karen Walker Cohn
Stephanie Bailey
LIFE/LOVE COACH
HTTPS://MISS-ADVENTURES.COM/

AUTHOR
VALERIE D. STATON

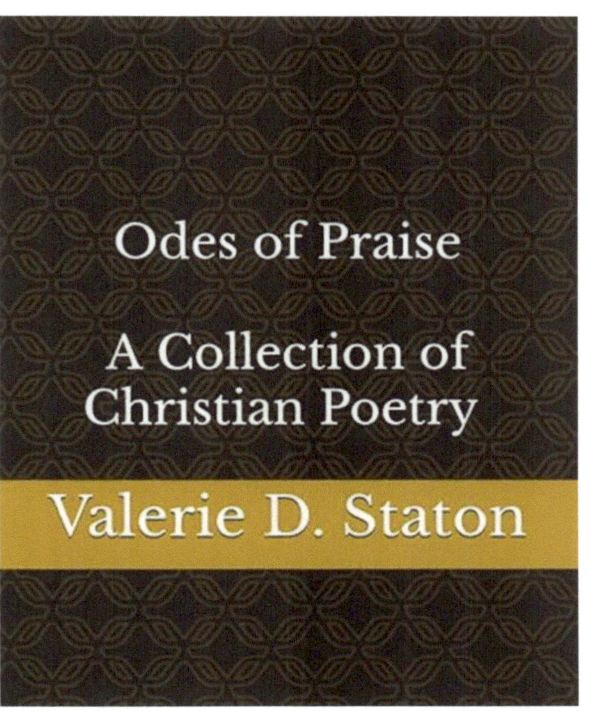

Odes of Praise: A Collection of Christian Poetry" is a Christian based book of poetry, edifying our Lord and Savior Jesus Christ for the good work He has done and continues to do in our lives each day. Topics include, sin, crucifixion, love, mercy, grace, redemption, sanctification, salvation, fellowship, worship, deliverance, and praise.

Valerie has contributed poetry in Haiku, 50 Haikus, and Three Line Poetry journals published by Prolific Press and in the following poetic anthologies: PS: It's Poetry, Volume I, An Anthology of Eclectic Contemporary Poems Written by Poets from Around the Globe and PS: It's Still Poetry, Volume II, An Anthology of Eclectic Contemporary Poems Written by Poets from Around the Globe, published by Arczis Web Technologies, Inc. In her spare time the author likes to read, write, make jewelry and antique shop.

SHENITA L YELL

CO-AUTHOR

THE TARNISHED CROWN

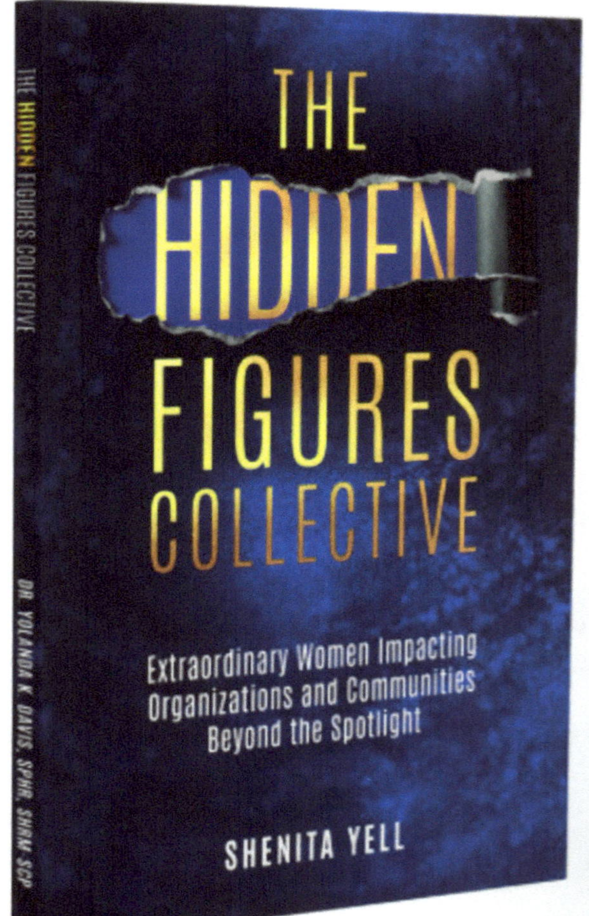

AUTHOR
Davina Ward

Davina Ward is an Author and Certified Christian Life Coach commissioned by God to free women and help them understand that resilience is possible - no matter what they have endured. She has experienced a vast array of challenges that have authenticated and motivated her to share her experiences with other vulnerable women.

She commonly refers to herself as the P.U.S.H. Coach, (Persist, Until, Satan, Halts), due to her effective coaching approach that guides women into learning how to discover and tap into their purpose through the tearing down of their limiting beliefs and insecurities.

Her program and teachings provide strategies to remove layers of lies, doubt, and shame that paralyze women of purpose.

Davina partners with her clients as they shift their focus from the reflection they see in the mirror to the warrior God designed them to be in the spirit. Her main goal is personal development leaving her clients feeling equipped and worthy to walk into what God has purposed them to do and be.

Her true passion lies in walking beside vulnerable women to awaken their inner selves as they enter into their destiny.

In addition to her life's work, Davina has an extensive background in the public sector working with individuals with modest means. She was born and raised in New Jersey and resides with her husband, Reverend Robert Ward. She delights in being a mother to 3 sons and a grandmother to 2 grandchildren. She delights in serving in her local church and community.

Tips for Developing Characters
Choosing Your Genre and Story

Creating compelling characters is one of the fundamental aspects of storytelling. Whether you're writing a novel, a screenplay, or even a short story, the characters you create will significantly impact your audience's connection to the narrative. Understanding the relationship between your genre, your story, and your character development can foster stronger and more relatable characters. Here are some insights and tips to help guide you through this creative process.

Choosing Your Genre

1. Understand Genre Expectations

Each genre has its conventions and expectations. For instance, in fantasy, readers anticipate elements like magical creatures and grand quests, while in romance, character chemistry and emotional arcs take center stage. Familiarizing yourself with the genre's norms will help you craft multifaceted characters that align with your chosen setting.

2. Tailor Characters to Genre

Once you have selected your genre, think about the types of characters that inhabit that world. In horror, for example, protagonists often display qualities of vulnerability or resilience, while antagonists may embody terror or the unknown. In a mystery genre, characters often have sharp intellects and unique backgrounds that lend themselves to investigative pursuits. Make sure your characters fit naturally within the genre to create authenticity.

Choosing Your Story

1. Define the Core Conflict

Understanding the central conflict of your story is crucial to character development. How do your characters react to this conflict? Are they proactive or reactive? For instance, in a dystopian novel, you may create a character who initially submits to authority but evolves into a rebellious figure. Their growth can be reflected through the development of their beliefs, fears, and relationships.

2. Create Backstories That Matter

Every character comes with a history that shapes their motivations and behavior. Craft backstories that inform your character's decisions and shape their arcs. Ensure that these backstories resonate with the central themes of your story, allowing their past experiences to influence their present actions. For example, a character driven by revenge in a thriller may have a traumatic history that explains their obsession.

Tips for Developing Characters
Choosing Your Genre and Story (Cont'd)

3. Develop Relationships

How characters interact with one another can significantly affect their development. Consider crafting complex relationships that evolve alongside the story. Dynamic interactions can highlight different facets of a character's personality, be it loyalty, betrayal, or love. For example, a hero may be challenged by a mentor figure, forcing them to confront their own weaknesses as the plot unfolds.

4. Use Character Arcs

A character arc is the transformation or inner journey of a character throughout the story. Whether they experience a positive transformation, a downfall, or remain static, clarity in their arc helps enhance your narrative. Establish clear motives, challenges, and resolutions that reflect their journey, making sure it aligns with your story's overall themes.

5. Ask Questions

Diving deeper into character development requires asking the right questions. What drives your character? What are their fears? What do they care about most? Use these questions to explore their motivations and develop their personalities. These inquiries will not only help flesh out your characters but also ensure that they are engaging and relatable to your audience.

6. Embrace Flaws and Strengths

Perfect characters can often come across as unrealistic. Instead, create characters with a blend of strengths and weaknesses that makes them relatable and memorable. Flaws can serve as obstacles that lead to growth, while strengths can be noteworthy traits that offer hope or inspiration. Balancing these attributes ensures characters are well-rounded and engaging.

Conclusion

In character development, understanding your genre and the storyline contributes greatly to the depth of your characters. Focus on genre expectations and conventions while also allowing room for creativity and crossovers. Your story's conflict, backstories, relationships, character arcs, and realistic imperfections can help you create authentic and engaging characters that resonate with your audience. As you embark on your writing journey, remember: characters are the heart of your story. Nurturing them thoughtfully can lead to a narrative that is not only compelling but also deeply moving. Happy writing!

Avalon Brown, #1 bestselling author hailing from Newark, NJ, has crafted a legacy through heartwarming children's books featuring her own grandchildren. Beyond her literary prowess, Avalon boasts a remarkable 42-year nursing career, specializing in GI/GU post-op, dialysis, and home care. Holding various titles, including Charge Nurse and Clinical Manager, she recently retired in April 2023 as an Infection Control Preventionist.

Avalon, is a member of the American Nurses Association and Women of Excellence Recognized. She earned her LPN at Essex County Tech, her ASN at Essex County College, and BSN at Regis University

Her diverse literary contributions also include a spiritual poetry book, a bishop's biography, a nursing memoir, and co-authorship in nine anthologies. Including her own anthology Nursing Is Our Passion "We Can't Quit."

14

Author: Avalon Brown
CONT'D

These are the compelling nursing books by Author Avalon Soulette Brown, a seasoned nurse and author. These books delve into the raw, real-life struggles and personal challenges faced by Avalon and other nurses. Shedding light on the emotional resilience required in the profession. With stories from Avalon and fellow nurses, these books provide both inspiration and practical guidance for managing the highs and lows of nursing. It is ideal for those at any stage of their career. Avalon books offer an honest look into nursing and essential insights for thriving in this demanding field.

FEATURED
AUTHOR

Dr. Jerwanda Johnson

To overcome, to go against and to go beyond is the mission. A self-motivator, optimistic, and conqueror ready to face any struggle without turning back; I am Dr. Jai, a graduate from Chatham University and a Medical Provider at my very own clinic. My greatest strength as an individual is my ability to connect with people. Surviving heartaches, devastating events, and living in darkness has painted a vivid image of who I am today. At an early age, these catastrophic events paved my path to destiny. Having compassion for others will always be the goal, as I continue this journey, we call LIFE.

As an Author, I will continue to embrace my visions through INK because there is someone out there who needs to know that obstacles should not make you give up. Many have asked me this question several times "Since you have faced so many devasting obstacles, how can you still smile and embrace life itself. Of course, my response is one must trust the process by keeping faith and believing in self. That is why God's guidance is the foundation. Here is a message to all Authors: writing is a process, but each stage prepares you for an experience towards success, therefore, keep writing. At an early age, my father introduced me to entrepreneurship. He always told me that it is all right to work for others but always have your OWN. And I knew all too well the lesson of sacrificing my needs out of responsibility or guilt. I did not want to fall back into the trap of believing that tough circumstances were signs of my worthlessness. But I still was not sure what to do. How could I use my education and degrees and have a fulfilling career that lit me up each day? I prayed some more. That is when I thought of starting an after-hours urgent and primary care clinic. Being in the medical field, I understood the need for such a practice and had the experience and desire to make it a reality.I have always been fascinated with fashions as a young teen. Style always conveys a message without having to say anything. I have modeled in different events starting when I was in college. As years have gone by the love for fashion continues to bring a burning desire within. As for the photoshoots I have done and am still doing, the love for fashion is embraced. Photoshoots for me allow me to enter another realm of self-awareness, self-confidence, and self-control. I love the creativity within the photoshoots. The beauty of doing these shoots allows me to present myself to others on a whole level of who I am. Lastly, the most important thing is what we create in the end and if we create that sense of awe in another person when all is through. No one says in a eulogy, "I loved that she took such an efficient path in life. What a great person." But they will say something like, "Her life was hard. I do not know how she did it, but her strength inspired me." That is the difference between purpose and path. My path may be forgotten, but the purpose will live on in the hearts of everyone it touches. We live our purpose when we move through the struggles – no matter what – when the goal seems impossible, and somehow, we keep plodding along.

A Letter to Myself!

Here is a letter to Myself reminding me why I am who I am.

Life has a funny way of showing you the choices you make, the thoughts you birth, and the action you produce... shapes you. "She comes from a loving home and The family is filled with love, laughter, and lessons. She works hard towards her dreams. whilst trying not to lose the unique parts of herself. She loves hard too. Dedicates and gives to loves that are wrong, painful, and suffocating. Still from the ashes of that time she regains strength, renewal of self and more self-love than what was lost. But most importantly a reverberant designed woman was in the making. Through endings come new beginnings. To love again and be loved past heartbreaks. and life's beatdowns was her focus. Her children, her family and being able to help. someone, even if just one life was impacted, was her passion. Still life threw endless. obstacles her way. Tornado sized storms hurrled fake loves, trying to rip at the success of her career. At times she felt alone, the darkness overshadowing the light of her successes. She marched on concealing the endless struggles while achieving. her dreams. She mentored, coached, and inspired many nurses to go further than what was before them. She was overcoming the losses that wanted her to suffer. and take away her wins. She continues to journey on growing, giving, loving, receiving, losing, and evolving herself. Photoshoots, click work the camera. Highlighting her striking beauty while concealing the hurt, and pain that churned, crippling her at times months on end. Outside, she was flawless. On the inside a darkness was threatening to overtake the very woman she was becoming. Her Niche is medicine. Her purpose is Loving Life while Helping Others. Still, she rises, in Spite of.

By: Dr. Jai Johnson

Behind
THE MASK
MY JOURNEY
Entrepreneurs:
Creating Legacies While
Embracing Our Journeys
Dr. Jerwanda Johnson DNP, FNP-C, LNC & Co-Authors

HOW TO
START UP A
Clinic
Making the impossible become possible
DR. JERWANDA JOHNSON DNP, FNP-C, LNC

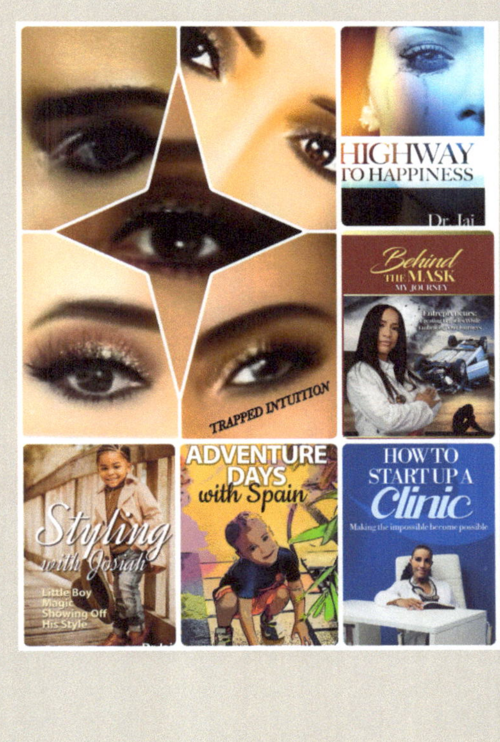

HIGHWAY
TO HAPPINESS
Dr. Jai
Behind
THE MASK
MY JOURNEY
TRAPPED INTUITION
Styling
with Josiah
Little Boy
Magic
Showing Off
His Style
ADVENTURE
DAYS
with Spain
HOW TO
START UP A
Clinic
Making the impossible become possible

ADVENTURE DAYS
with Spain
Dr. Jai

Love HAS NO
BOUNDARIES
A Story Of Friendship & Hope
ROSS SWANN

Styling
with Josiah
Little Boy
Magic
Showing Off
His Style
Dr. Jai

HIGHWAY
TO HAPPINESS
Dr. Jai

WHAT'S COOKING FOR THE HOLIDAYS?

#1 ROASTED CHRISTMAS TURKEY DINNER

Ingredients:

- 1 whole turkey (12-14 lbs)
- 1/2 cup unsalted butter, softened
- 1 tablespoon garlic powder
- 1 tablespoon onion powder
- 1 tablespoon dried thyme
- 2 teaspoons salt
- 1 teaspoon black pepper
- 2 cups chicken broth
- 1 lemon, halved
- 1 onion, quartered
- 4 sprigs of fresh rosemary
- 4 sprigs of fresh thyme

Instructions:

1. Preheat the oven to 325°F (165°C).
2. Rinse the turkey and pat dry.
3. Mix butter, garlic powder, onion powder, dried thyme, salt, and pepper. Rub the mixture under and over the turkey skin.
4. Stuff the cavity with lemon, onion, rosemary, and thyme.
5. Place turkey on a roasting rack in a pan. Add chicken broth to the bottom.
6. Roast for 3 to 3.5 hours, basting every 30 minutes, until the internal temperature reaches 165°F (74°C).
7. Let rest for 30 minutes before carving.

RECIPE # 2
CHEESY CHRISTMAS CASSEROLE

Ingredients:

- 3 cups cooked broccoli florets

- 2 cups cooked rice

- 1 can cream of mushroom soup (10.5 oz)

- 1 cup sour cream

- 1/2 teaspoon garlic powder

- 1/2 teaspoon onion powder

- 2 cups shredded cheddar cheese

- 1/2 cup bread crumbs

- 2 tablespoons butter, melted

Instructions:

1. Preheat oven to 350°F (175°C).

2. In a large bowl, mix broccoli, rice, soup, sour cream, garlic powder, onion powder, and 1.5 cups of cheddar cheese.

3. Spread the mixture into a greased casserole dish.

4. Top with remaining cheese. Mix bread crumbs and butter, then sprinkle on top.

5. Bake for 25-30 minutes, until bubbly and golden.

#3. CHRISTMAS CHOCOLATE YULE LOG DESSERT

Ingredients:

- 5 large eggs, separated
- 1/2 cup granulated sugar
- 1/4 cup unsweetened cocoa powder
- 1/4 cup all-purpose flour
- 1 teaspoon vanilla extract
- 1/4 teaspoon salt

For Filling and Frosting:

- 1 cup heavy whipping cream
- 2 tablespoons powdered sugar
- 1 teaspoon vanilla extract
- 1/2 cup chocolate ganache or frosting

Instructions:

1. Preheat oven to 350°F (175°C). Line a jelly roll pan with parchment.
2. Beat egg yolks and sugar until thick and pale. Add cocoa powder, flour, vanilla, and salt.
3. Beat egg whites to stiff peaks and fold into the yolk mixture. Spread batter into the pan.
4. Bake for 12 minutes. Turn onto a towel and roll gently.
5. Unroll, spread whipped cream (whipped with sugar and vanilla), and reroll. Frost with ganache.
6. Decorate as desired and chill before serving.

Literary
MOMENTS & RESOURCES

A One-Stop Shop
For Authors

Lead by Prof. Paulette Henson and Michelle Hardy (@SolitudeWithMichelle)

At BWA, our goal is to educate new and blossoming writers on how to write and publish books.

Whether you are just budding, wanting to finally complete a writing project, or already seasoned, we're more than happy to help you on your journey from writing to publishing your book.

BWA proudly announces its first course to help our strong community build the best possible quality book for its members and their target audience. Author Preneurship 101 taught by Professor Paulette Henson and Michelle Hardy is an author business writing course designed to help new and seasoned authors get published in a one-stop shop. Being a new author can be challenging, but BWA is here to make things go as smoothly as possible with a complete writing and publishing process.
For information or to register send an email to:

Education@blackwomenauthors.net

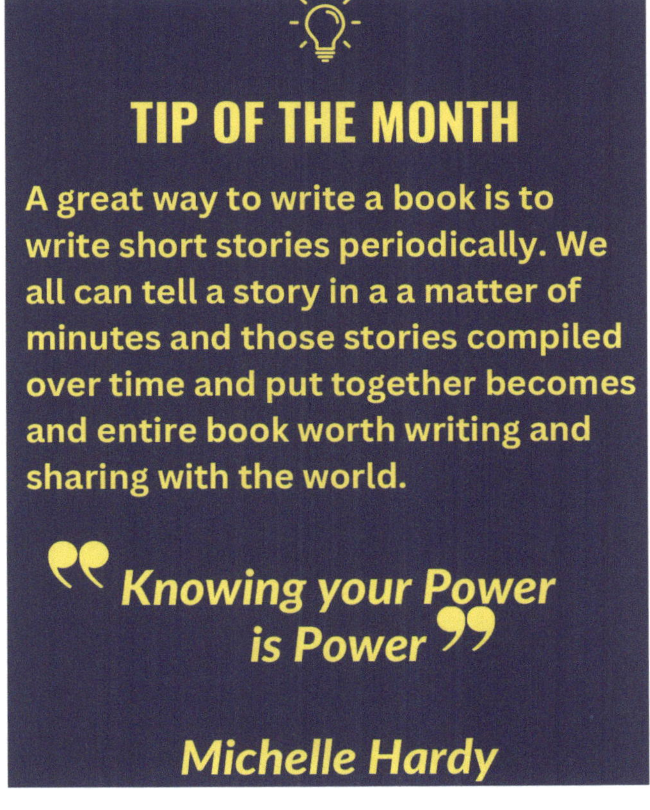

We Help
You Promote Your Business & Books

PUBLICATION & MARKETING COMPANY

SERVICES

Book Promotion & Strategy

Marketing in one of our monthly BWA publications.

Digital Book & Author Development

Website Design & Development
Book Trailers
Print to Ebook Conversion

Education & Resources

New Author Course & Workshop
Online Courses for Seasoned Authors

ABOUT US

We are committed to being the primary resource for Authors to succeed in their Book Promotions.

WHY CHOOSE US ?

We are the only Black Owned platform providing this level of resource and service.

CONTACT

BWAMAGAZINE@GMAIL.COM

blackwomenauthors.net

Health Notes

The Spiritual Meaning Of The Holidays!

As the end of the year approaches, the holiday season brings with it a time of reflection, renewed connection, and hopeful anticipation. At the heart of this special time lies the spiritual meaning that transcends any single religion or cultural tradition. The essence of the holidays is the spirit of loving one another. Whether it's the Christian celebration of Christmas, the African American tradition of Kwanzaa, or the universal joy of welcoming a new year, the common thread is an emphasis on community, compassion, and our shared humanity.

During Christmas, the birth of Jesus Christ symbolizes the divine gift of unconditional love. Kwanzaa honors the seven principles of African heritage, including unity, self-determination, and faith. And as we say goodbye to the old year, the arrival of a new one represents an opportunity for fresh starts and bold resolutions.

Across these diverse observances, the holiday spirit encourages us to look beyond our differences and find common ground. It's a chance to slow down, express gratitude, and recommit ourselves to the values that truly matter - kindness, generosity, and the belief that we are all connected.

As 2024 draws to a close, the spiritual meaning of the season invites us to reflect on the year gone by. What lessons have we learned? How can we grow and improve in the years ahead? By tapping into the universal themes of light, renewal, and goodwill, we can enter 2025 with a sense of purpose and optimism.

This is the perfect time to set meaningful goals for the new year - whether it's practicing more mindfulness, volunteering in our communities, or finding innovative ways to make a positive impact. When we approach the future with open hearts and a genuine commitment to one another, we unlock the fullest expression of the holiday spirit.

No matter our faith or background, the end-of-year festivities remind us that we are all part of the human family. As we celebrate and look forward, may we carry this sense of connection, compassion, and hope with us, not just for the holidays, but throughout the year to come.

Good Health!

P.K. Wilson

FLIGHTS - HOTELS - CAR RENTALS

CRUISES - VACATION PACKAGES

- BUSINESS & PERSONAL TRAVEL
- FAMILY/HOLIDAY EVENTS
- BOOK FAIRS
- ADVENTURE TRAVEL
- SPECIAL & CUSTOM PACKAGES

Priceless Little Things!

Just staying busy in the day-to-day, I became remiss about how much our babies and small people mimic what we do. Their minds are constantly recording what we do, how we say, how we act, our tone, and so on. Lucky for me, I am a positive person, most of my habits are good, and most of the time I know they're watching me (and learning).

Kids love to have a book read to them. Read to them with enthusiasm and expression as much as possible. Then, later, ask them simple questions about the story, like what was his/her name? Or, why did that happen?

I remember reading the three little pigs to my sons when they were toddlers. I used different voices for each pig, and another voice for the big bad wolf. Then I would re-read the book while pointing at the words so they also recognized sight words. Soon enough it was easy for them to read a story back to me.

Nowadays, I let my one-year-old granddaughter walk around the library freely in the sections appropriate for her age. I'll point at a familiar book and ask her "what's that one"?

Forgetting about her 'inside' library voice she'll turn to me and yell out whatever the story is, mimicking the full effects of the voices in the story. She is eager to let me know she knows the story, even though her vocabulary is primarily baby words.

Now, the lesson here is to always be mindful that these small people are recording and mimicking everything. They develop excellent reading habits and a love for books. This is good.

The best part of this short story is my one-year-old granddaughter now has a new baby sister who is only a few months old. It is priceless to hear the toddler telling stories to the new baby, albeit in her own baby speak, mimicking the same voices and sounds that I make.

You can't put a price on that!

By A. Williams

QR CODE - A POWERFUL TOOL FOR AUTHORS
By Valerie D. Staton

QR codes have emerged as a powerful tool for authors looking to enhance their promotional materials and connect with their audience in a more engaging way. One of the primary benefits of incorporating QR codes into promotional materials, such as bookmarks, flyers, or posters, is the ease of access they provide to digital content. By scanning a QR code, readers can instantly access the author's website, social media profiles, or additional resources like sample chapters or exclusive interviews. This seamless transition from print to digital enhances reader engagement and can lead to increased book sales or event attendance.

Moreover, QR codes offer authors a unique opportunity to track engagement and gather data. By using different QR codes for various promotional efforts, authors can analyze which materials are most effective in driving traffic to their online platforms. This valuable insight allows for more targeted marketing strategies, enabling authors to refine their approach and better connect with potential readers. In a competitive literary market, the ability to adapt and optimize promotional efforts based on real-time feedback is a significant advantage.

Lastly, QR codes give authors the chance to create dynamic, interactive experiences that can captivate tech-savvy readers. For instance, authors can link QR codes to multimedia content, such as book trailers, podcasts, or even virtual events. This interactivity not only enriches the reader's experience but also helps authors stand out in an increasingly digital world. As promotional landscapes evolve, the implementation of QR codes represents a smart innovation, merging traditional marketing with modern technology to foster deeper connections with audiences.

The Author's Lounge
W/PAULETTE

Next Guest Author:
You!

PROMOTE YOUR BOOK !

FOR MORE DETAILS

EMAIL:THEAUTHORSLOUNGETVSHOW@GMAIL.COM

WATCH ON FACEBOOK
(LIVE) BLACK WOMEN
AUTHORS
& YOUTUBE

LIKE/COMMENT/SHARE/SUBSCRIBE

Strategies for Copyright Protection and Online Content Security in Book Publishing

today's digital age, where technology has revolutionized how we create, share, and consume content, the concept of pyright has never been more critical—especially in the realm of book publishing. As artificial intelligence (AI) and oth vanced technologies continue to shape the literary landscape, it's vital for authors, publishers, and content creators derstand both the challenges and the opportunities that lie ahead. This article delves into the complexities of pyright protection in the digital era, focusing on AI's role in content creation, the challenges of online infringement, d strategies to secure intellectual property rights effectively.

e Evolving Landscape of Copyright in Book Publishing

pyright has traditionally served as a legal framework that grants exclusive rights to creators, protecting their original rks from unauthorized use. However, the digital age has dramatically transformed this landscape, particularly in boo plishing. The ease with which digital content can be replicated and distributed without permission has made copyrig ringement a pervasive issue. For authors and publishers, protecting their works from piracy and unauthorized tribution is a growing concern.

e rapid advancements in AI have introduced new complexities to the copyright discussion. AI-generated content, for tance, raises questions about ownership and the extent to which copyright laws apply. As AI tools become more phisticated, they can generate text that closely resembles human writing, blurring the lines between original and ivative works. For book publishers, this means navigating uncharted waters where traditional copyright principles y not fully apply.

allenges of Copyright in the Digital Age

e of the primary challenges faced by copyright holders in the digital era is the sheer scale of content being produced d shared online. Every day, millions of new pieces of content are uploaded to the internet, making it nearly impossibl monitor and enforce copyright protections effectively. For authors and publishers, this can lead to rampant piracy, ere unauthorized copies of books are shared freely across platforms, undermining both the financial and creative ue of their work.

e anonymity of the internet further complicates the enforcement of copyright. Identifying and prosecuting infringers be a daunting task, often leading to a game of cat and mouse where infringers find new ways to circumvent legal ions. This is particularly problematic in the book publishing industry, where the unauthorized distribution of digital ks can happen across multiple platforms, from peer-to-peer sharing sites to social media.

e Role of Digital Rights Management (DRM)

ital Rights Management (DRM) has emerged as a key tool for protecting copyrighted content in the digital age. DRM hnologies allow authors and publishers to control how their digital works are accessed, copied, and distributed. For mple, DRM can restrict the number of times a digital book can be shared or limit access to only those who have chased the content legally.

ile DRM offers a level of protection, it is not without its drawbacks. Critics argue that DRM can be overly restrictive, netimes penalizing legitimate users who may face difficulties in accessing their

purchased content across different devices. Furthermore, determined infringers can often find ways to bypass D
protections, rendering them less effective in some cases. Nevertheless, for book publishers, DRM remains an
essential component of a broader strategy to protect intellectual property in the digital space.

Copyright and AI: Navigating New Challenges

The intersection of AI and copyright law presents new challenges for the publishing industry. AI-generated cont
raises fundamental questions about who owns the rights to these works. If an AI system creates a piece of text
is later published as a book, who holds the copyright—the developer of the AI, the user who inputted the data, o
AI itself?

Currently, copyright law does not fully account for works generated by non-human creators, leading to a legal g
area. This uncertainty can create potential conflicts over ownership and royalties, especially as AI tools become
more integrated into the writing and publishing process. For authors, understanding the implications of using AI
their creative process is crucial to ensuring that their rights are protected.

Strategies for Protecting Content Online

In light of these challenges, authors and publishers must adopt comprehensive strategies to protect their works
online. Here are several approaches that can help safeguard intellectual property in the digital age:

Watermarking and Metadata: Embedding digital watermarks and metadata into e-books can help track their
distribution and identify unauthorized copies. This technology allows publishers to monitor where their content
being shared and take action if necessary.

Monitoring and Enforcement: Regularly monitoring the internet for unauthorized copies of your work is essentia
Tools like web crawlers and content recognition software can help identify instances of infringement. Once
identified, authors and publishers should be prepared to take swift action, whether through cease-and-desist le
or legal proceedings.

Legal Safeguards: Working with legal professionals to draft clear terms of use and licensing agreements can hel
protect your work. These documents should explicitly state how your content can be used and outline the
consequences of unauthorized use.

Education and Awareness: Educating your audience about the importance of copyright and the consequences of
infringement can foster a culture of respect for intellectual property. This can be done through blog posts, socia
media campaigns, and even within the content of your books.

Leveraging Technology: Beyond DRM, other technologies like blockchain are being explored as potential solutio
for copyright protection. Blockchain can create an immutable record of ownership, making it easier to prove the
originality and authorship of digital works.

Copyright Licensing and Monetization in Book Publishing

In addition to protecting content, authors and publishers should also consider how to effectively license and
monetize their works in the digital age. Traditional publishing models may not be sufficient to address the
challenges posed by digital distribution, but new opportunities are emerging.

Creative Commons Licensing: One approach is to use Creative Commons licenses, which allow creators to grant
certain usage rights to the public while retaining copyright. This can help authors reach a wider audience while
maintaining control over their work.

ternative Revenue Streams: Exploring alternative revenue streams such as crowdfunding, bscriptions, and direct sales through online platforms can provide additional income while ducing reliance on traditional publishing models. For example, platforms like Patreon allow thors to build a community of supporters who contribute financially in exchange for exclusive ntent.

onclusion: Embracing the Future of Copyright in Publishing
the digital landscape continues to evolve, the publishing industry must adapt to new challenges d opportunities. Protecting intellectual property in the age of AI requires a multifaceted approach at combines legal safeguards, technology, and education. By staying informed and proactive, thors and publishers can navigate the complexities of copyright in the digital era, ensuring that eir creative works are protected and that they can continue to thrive in a rapidly changing vironment.
e future of copyright in book publishing lies in embracing these new technologies and strategies, t just as a means of protection, but as tools for innovation and growth. By understanding the tricacies of copyright in the digital age, creators can safeguard their work while also exploring w ways to reach and engage with their audience.

bout the Author
ctoria Pearson, a professional with a diverse background spanning 26 years in technology, lucation, entrepreneurship, and community service, is a passionate advocate for community npowerment and education. She has served on the boards of various non-for-profit organization d is a sought-after speaker and consultant. Pearson holds a bachelor's degree in psychology m UCLA and has completed concurrent master's-level studies in Health Administration and rontology. She is the founder of grokly.me, an innovative e-learning platform offering a diverse nge of courses from The Writer's Workshop which includes 35+ courses for self-published authors artificial intelligence, entrepreneurship, spirituality and wellness, personal growth, and integration for the formerly incarcerated. She is actively seeking partnerships with organizations d individuals who share her mission to democratize education and ignite passion for lifelong arning for disadvantaged persons. She can be reached at info@grokly.me.

Poetry is Life!

Poetry, often described as the language of the soul, has a unique ability to transcend time, culture, and circumstance, leaving an indelible mark on the hearts and minds of those who encounter its verses. Beyond the rhythmic words and metaphors lies a profound power that has shaped societies, moved nations, and connected individuals on a deeply emotional level. Let's delve into the mystical world of poetry and explore the extraordinary power it holds.

1. The Healing Elixir: Poetry possesses a remarkable therapeutic quality. In times of sorrow, it can be a soothing balm, offering solace and a means of expression for emotions too profound for ordinary words. The act of crafting verses can be cathartic, helping individuals process grief, anxiety, or even joy, and find inner peace through self-expression.

2. The Bridge Between Souls: Poetry has a unique ability to connect people across cultural, linguistic, and geographical divides. It transcends the boundaries of language, allowing individuals from diverse backgrounds to understand and empathize with one another's experiences. It serves as a universal language that reminds us of our shared humanity.

3. A Lens to the World: Poets often act as society's mirrors, reflecting its beauty, flaws, and contradictions. Through verse, they shed light on societal issues, injustices, and human conditions that might otherwise remain unseen. Poetry challenges the status quo and fosters a collective awareness, driving change and sparking movements for justice and equality.

4. The Dance of Imagination: Poetry is a playground for imagination. It encourages us to see the world through fresh eyes, to explore the mysteries of existence, and to question the norms of society. It unlocks the doors to creativity, inviting us to wander through the realms of fantasy and the possibilities of the unknown.

5. A Timeless Legacy: Poems are timeless treasures. The verses of poets from centuries past continue to resonate with readers today. The enduring quality of poetry lies in its ability to capture the essence of the human experience, making it relevant across generations and eras.

*6. **A Vehicle for Social Change:** Poetry has historically played a pivotal role in driving social change. Poets like Langston Hughes, Maya Angelou, and Pablo Neruda used their verses to advocate for civil rights, equality, and justice. Through their words, they ignited movements and inspired generations to stand up for what they believed in.

7. **The Elevation of Language: Poetry elevates language to an art form. It demonstrates the beauty of precision and the magic of metaphor. Poets carefully select words, creating a symphony of sounds and meanings that delight the senses and challenge the mind.

8. **An Echo of Identity: Poetry is a profound expression of identity. It allows individuals to embrace and celebrate their cultural heritage, personal experiences, and individual uniqueness. It serves as a repository of cultural memory, preserving traditions and stories for future generations.

In a world often dominated by prose and pragmatism, poetry stands as a testament to the enduring power of human creativity and expression. It serves as a bridge between hearts, a beacon of hope, and a catalyst for change. Through its profound ability to heal, connect, and inspire, poetry remains a force that continues to shape the world, one verse at a time.

Paulette
Henson

"SHE AROSE"
BY VALERIE D. STATON

She arose...
A phoenix out of a pile of ashes...
Out of abandonment,
Out of hardships and constraints,
Out of depression and sadness.

She arose...
Out of cutbacks and setbacks...
Taking to the sky, looking down on ghosts,
of mental, physical and economical abuse.

She arose...
Strong, majestic, empowered and divine!
Out of trials and tribulations she climbed...
Casting off unsightly remnants of loss and despair,
Leaving pain and sadness behind.

She arose...
A new creature – beautiful and refined!
Out of a pile of ashes the phoenix climbed,
With a surge of energy, she took to the sky,
And never looked back where her burdens lie.

She arose!

This 40-page story is a metaphorical gem.

It is a journey for your senses, and it is worth taking!

This is my gift to anyone who has ever experienced losing a loved one.

By Stella Stella

The South Side Of Heaven

Stella Stella

Many required readings in college included commonly known American Literaries (i.e. Hemingway, Poe, Steinbeck, Wells, etc.). All were great writers and I have no knocks against them. However, their stories were too abstract for my life. Within the realm of Literature, there is room for those/us who have a different background, a different perspective, and a passion for reading and writing".

Dr. Lisa L. Campbell

Dr. Lisa L. Campbell, known as "The Growth Motivator™," is the author of the inspirational book "Grow With Me." In this book, Dr. Lisa shares her journey of overcoming significant personal and professional challenges. Through vivid storytelling and heartfelt reflections, she shares her life lessons on resilience, faith, and personal growth. Her journey as an author began with a desire to inspire others, and she has developed a motivational writing style that connects deeply with readers. "Grow With Me" encourages readers to shed the weight of their burdens, embrace change, and pursue their dreams with determination and confidence. Dr. Lisa's engaging narrative and genuine voice make her book an uplifting and transformative read.

GROW
WITH
ME
THE JOURNAL

OVERCOME CHALLENGES, EMBRACE
AUTHENTICITY, AND CULTIVATE GROWTH

DR. LISA L CAMPBELL®

Photography by Craig A. Kirkland
Great Amazement Multimedia Entertainment LLC

Native New Yorker Living in Rhode Island Celebrates the Success of Her First Book

CLARISE ANNETTE BROOKS knew from a young age that she could spark magic when she put pen to paper. "I recall when our teachers would give us creative writing assignments in elementary school. We each had to take turns reading our work at the front of the room. My classmates often requested that I go first," Clarise recalls. "I knew I had them when they laughed at the right moment, gasped at the right time, and talked with me later about the characters I had created or about the poetry that I had just performed for them. It came easy to me and I enjoyed it SO MUCH. It has always been fun to use imagery to create a scene, alliteration to develop a flow of words, or repetition to demand emphasis. These tools of the language helped me to take my classmates on a journey with me and planted the seed for my lifelong love of performing my work before a live audience. I learned how to use language and its tools to touch the minds and spirits of others."

AUTHOR

CHANTELLE CROWELL

My first self-published book, entitled *We Wake Up*, was inspired by my children. They encouraged me to write it, helping me transform my ideas into reality and fulfill my dreams.

My eighth book, *We Are the Revolution*, powerfully reflects our life's journey. It demonstrates that despite obstacles, we must keep our heads up, pursue our dreams, and let nothing or no one stand in the way of achieving our goals.

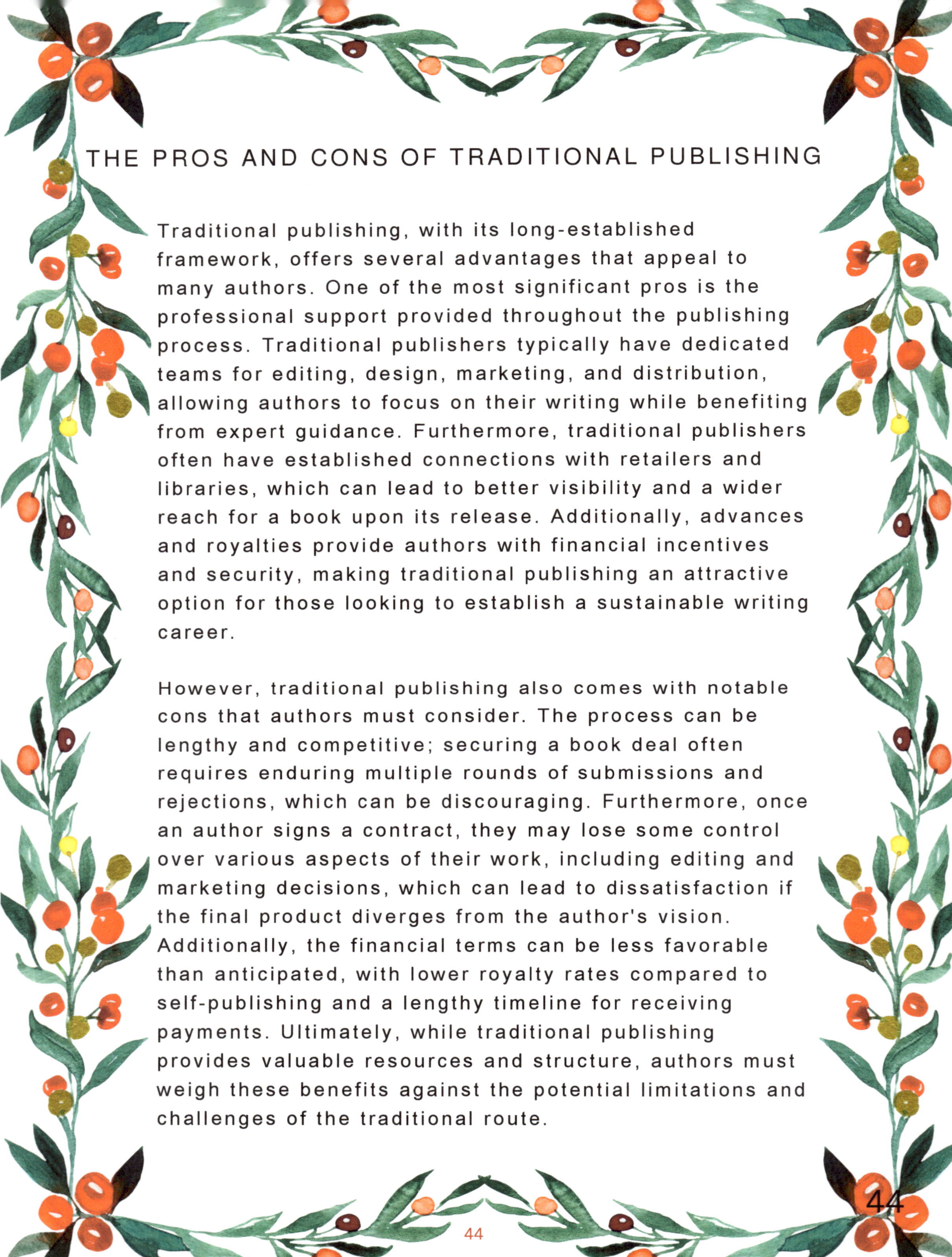

THE PROS AND CONS OF TRADITIONAL PUBLISHING

Traditional publishing, with its long-established framework, offers several advantages that appeal to many authors. One of the most significant pros is the professional support provided throughout the publishing process. Traditional publishers typically have dedicated teams for editing, design, marketing, and distribution, allowing authors to focus on their writing while benefiting from expert guidance. Furthermore, traditional publishers often have established connections with retailers and libraries, which can lead to better visibility and a wider reach for a book upon its release. Additionally, advances and royalties provide authors with financial incentives and security, making traditional publishing an attractive option for those looking to establish a sustainable writing career.

However, traditional publishing also comes with notable cons that authors must consider. The process can be lengthy and competitive; securing a book deal often requires enduring multiple rounds of submissions and rejections, which can be discouraging. Furthermore, once an author signs a contract, they may lose some control over various aspects of their work, including editing and marketing decisions, which can lead to dissatisfaction if the final product diverges from the author's vision. Additionally, the financial terms can be less favorable than anticipated, with lower royalty rates compared to self-publishing and a lengthy timeline for receiving payments. Ultimately, while traditional publishing provides valuable resources and structure, authors must weigh these benefits against the potential limitations and challenges of the traditional route.

THE PROS AND CONS OF SELF-PUBLISHING

Self-publishing has emerged as a popular alternative to traditional publishing, offering numerous benefits that attract many aspiring authors. One of the primary advantages is the level of creative control it affords writers. Self-published authors retain ownership of their work and can make decisions about content, cover design, and marketing strategies. This independence often leads to a more personal and authentic expression of their vision. Additionally, self-publishing can be financially rewarding; authors can set their own prices and keep a higher percentage of the royalties compared to traditional publishing contracts. With the rise of digital platforms, reaching a global audience has become easier than ever, allowing authors to bypass the barriers of traditional publishing gatekeepers.

However, self-publishing also comes with its challenges. One major drawback is the increased responsibility placed on the author; they must manage all aspects of the publishing process, from editing to marketing, which can be overwhelming, especially for those lacking experience in these areas. Without the backing of a traditional publisher, self-published authors may find it difficult to achieve widespread recognition or to secure a spot in larger distribution channels, potentially limiting their book's visibility. Moreover, the self-publishing landscape is crowded, making it essential for authors to invest time and resources into effective marketing strategies to stand out. In summary, while self-publishing offers remarkable opportunities for creative freedom and financial gain, it also requires a significant commitment of time and effort, along with the ability to navigate an often competitive market and challenges of the traditional route.

YOUR NEXT BEST READ IS HERE!

The HER•ology of A Woman
by Dr. Shamarah J. Hutchins

A MUST-READ FOR EVERYONE!

This page-turning memoir, which covers the gamut of recovery from multiple rounds of setbacks, will leave the reader inspired by a woman who draws from her own armor of experiences to assist her clients in healing.

WWW.THEMINDOLOGISTDOC.COM

AUTHOR
OMEAKIO TUCKER

Bio

Omeakio Tucker, a new and upcoming author, fearlessly shares her personal journey of facing challenges, feeling stuck, and ultimately breaking free in her transformative book. Drawing from her own experiences and her deep connection with God, Omeakio is your cheerleader and guide, showing you that transformation is possible. This book is more than just another self-help guide; it's a heart-to-heart conversation and a loving reminder that you are capable of so much more than you ever thought possible. Omeakio will help you identify the limiting beliefs and patterns that have been holding you back and provide you with the tools you need to unleash your Unstoppable PowHer.

47

Is He Your Holiday Man?

When I was growing up, my dad loved holidays. To him, holidays like Easter, Thanksgiving, and Christmas meant bringing family and friends together around the dining room table, which was always beautifully set with fine china, silverware, and holiday decorations. My parents would prepare and cook the night before, and my mom would make her famous homemade sweet potato pies that our neighbors drooled with anticipation and looked forward to. Our home would radiate with holiday cheer, mainly during Christmas when my dad would stream lights inside and outside our house. We would decorate the house and watch holiday movies together as a family.

On Christmas morning, my dad would make his special homemade blueberry pancakes while playing Gladys Knight and the Pips' record. Whenever his favorite song, "Midnight Train to Georgia," played, he would sing and dance in the kitchen with my mom, encouraging us to join in. As my siblings and I got older, we all helped set the table and decorate—the tree being my favorite. Although my mom enjoyed the holidays, my dad was the driving force behind our traditions.

As I grew older, the importance of holidays became more significant.

Thirty-four years ago, when my dad passed away, our family's holiday traditions faded. My mom moved to another state for a job, and my siblings and I were spread out in different states for college, making it difficult for all of us to be together for every holiday.

As I got older, I realized how important it is to be with someone who also enjoys holidays, especially since these are the times I miss my dad the most. Fortunately, most men I dated were open to celebrating or sharing my love for the holidays. However, there were a few men who were not.

Here's the thing: Some men don't acknowledge holidays for religious reasons or negative past experiences. Others may become stressed and less enthusiastic about creating a festive experience. However, some men may not be as passionate about the holidays as you are but will fully support your excitement and make your holiday meaningful. My favorite is the group of men who love the holidays more than you and make an extra effort to celebrate, making you feel appreciated and special.

A "holiday enthusiast" embraces the holiday spirit and supports your traditions.

Not everyone loves the holidays, and that's okay. If holidays and traditions are essential to you, ask important questions.

I met a man who happily supports his wife's love for holidays. She enjoys decorating and does not skimp on spreading her holiday cheer. They even have a large shed for her collections of holiday decorations she has (and keeps) collected over the years. His wife will decorate their entire home, inside, outside, and on the front lawn, for Valentine's Day, Easter, Saint Patrick's Day, the 4th of July, Thanksgiving, Christmas, and New Year's Eve. Despite not being as enthusiastic as his wife, he finds pure joy in seeing her excitement. He helps her find decorations and gifts throughout the year, making it their unique tradition—which fills him with happiness.

Having a partner who supports and works hard to make holidays (whichever one you enjoy) special is essential—even if they do not share your level of enthusiasm.

Some men may end up enjoying holidays because of you.

I was in a relationship with a man who initially didn't enjoy the holidays due to negative experiences from his past. However, because he knew I enjoyed celebrating, he made an effort to make the holidays special, and we created beautiful memories together.

Some men can bring holiday cheer into your life and change your feelings about holidays—or enhance them, just like my dad did for me.

My current partner and his sons love the holidays, and we've created our own traditions while incorporating some of my dad's. We have holiday parties and family dinners and decorate our tree and home while sipping eggnog and listening to holiday music. We watch various holiday movies in our holiday onesies, and my favorite is that on Christmas morning, my partner makes blueberry pancakes while playing *Gladys Knight and the Pip's* hits. When the song "Midnight Train to Georgia" plays, my partner even slow dances with me to honor my dad's memory.

If you enjoy celebrating the holidays, having a partner who shares your enthusiasm is essential.

Ladies, whether it's spending quality time with loved ones (or your furbaby), reflecting on what you're grateful for, or simply embracing the festive spirit, having a partner who values the holidays can bring more joy, love, and sparkle into your life. Look for someone open to spreading holiday cheer and making the season everything you dream of or more.

49

Love, Romance, & Friendship

(with a Twist)

Prepare to have your own paradigms challenged.

A timeless story of Love, Romance, and Friendship. Follow the journey of sixty-one-year-old, Tina Mason, as she navigates the loss of her husband. On the same day of his funeral, a knock at the door presents her with a quandary – a different opportunity to grieve.

PS – If this was a screenplay, I know who I would cast. Who would you cast?

50

IN THIS EDITION...

BWA TEAM

Paulette Henson - CEO, Founder
Denise L - Design
Felicia K - Administrative
Khoury S - Technical
Michelle H - Education
Taryn L - Operations
Valerie S - Editing
Taniesha C-P - Contributor
Talona C - Contributor

51